KEYBOARD COOKBOOK

Text by Jana Ranson

Music by the Editors at Hal Leonard Corporation

ISBN 0-634-06213-1

HAL•LEONARD® CORPORATION

7777 W. BLUEMOUND RD. P.O. BOX 13819 MILWAUKEE, WI 53213

In Australia Contact:
Hal Leonard Australia Pty. Ltd.
22 Taunton Drive P.O. Box 5130
Cheltenham East, 3192 Victoria, Australia
Email: ausadmin@halleonard.com

Visit Hal Leonard Online at
www.halleonard.com

CONTENTS

Although donning an apron is optional, once you've sampled each and every entrée within the *Keyboard Cookbook*, the stylistic spicing-up of your playing will be inevitable! Featured here are 40 style-specific, user-friendly, cookbook-format musical recipes from eight essential musical categories—blues, country, jazz, Latin, popular, R&B, and traditional. The *Keyboard Cookbook* will make you a master chef of a wide variety of musical styles in no time.

Each recipe featured in the *Keyboard Cookbook* is organized as follows:

- **Introduction:** A brief description and history of the featured style.
- **Time:** The time at which the featured recipe should be cooked (i.e., 4/4 time).
- **Yield:** The quantity of the featured style (i.e., twelve measures of swingin' blues).
- **Ingredients:** The elements critical to the playing of the featured recipe, including instructions as to their correct and most effective execution.
- **For Best Results:** The sound settings at which to "cook" the featured recipe for the most authentic result (i.e., electric piano sound, Hammond organ sound, tack hammers, etc.).
- **Spice It Up:** Suggestions to further elaborate upon and add pizzazz to the featured recipe.
- **Sample the Recipes of These Leading Chefs of the Style:** A few of the most notable artists of the featured style.
- **Recipe:** A musical example of the featured style.

It is also important to note that a number of the styles featured in the *Keyboard Cookbook* do not customarily feature keyboard instrumentation. Therefore, the artists listed in the "Sample the Recipes of These Leading Chefs of the Style" sections may be musicians other than keyboardists, especially if no popular keyboard players have recorded as specialists in that particular style. Nevertheless, the reader is encouraged to seek out recordings by the artists listed so as to get the overall flavor of these styles. In addition, it should be stressed that the recipes for those styles that are not, by convention, keyboard-inclusive have been fully interpreted and adapted for the solo keyboardist. Every single style, regardless of its degree of keyboard incorporation, is now an option for you!

So be creative, have fun, and get cookin'!

BOOGIE WOOGIE

The boogie woogie is a blues piano style that was first developed around 1936, and reached its commercial pinnacle in the 1940s. This jazz-influenced idiom was a favorite among early R&B and rock 'n' roll musicians whose songs were often infused with boogie's elements—in particular, its walking bass line. The style's popularity held throughout the 1950s and continues to shape music today.

Time
4/4

Yield
Twelve measures of a somewhat flashier, extemporaneous alternative to the more traditional blues styles.

Ingredients
- A fairly bright tempo that should be played faster than traditional blues.
- A left-hand ostinato which is the most important characteristic of the style. Let it drive the tune.
- Rhythm and pulse to be emphasized over melody.
- Mandatory (read: important and essential!) right-hand grace notes featured on beat 1 of each measure. Trill/tremolo the long notes. The right hand should be ornamental.
- Swing it or play it "straight."

For Best Results
Dial up a honky-tonk piano sound with a "room" reverb to simulate the sound of an early recording.

Spice It Up
- Add polyrhythmic right-hand improvisations.
- Substitute an 8- or 16-bar progression for the 12-bar.
- When repeating, rest one hand for 2-4 bars to give it a break and let the other take over.

Sample the Recipes of These Leading Chefs of the Style
Albert Ammons, Charles "Cow Cow" Davenport, Pete Johnson, Meade "Lux" Lewis, Clarence "Pine Top" Smith, Jimmy Yancey.

BOOGIE WOOGIE

TRACK 1

DELTA BLUES

With origins in the deep south of Mississippi, the delta blues reflects the fiery, languorous, and sweltering climate of its birthplace. Developed foremost as a solo-guitar blues form, the style was also frequently performed by full-string orchestras, making it a naturally translatable idiom for other melodic instruments such as keyboards.

Time
4/4

Yield
Twelve measures of the blues genre's most passionately languid style.

Ingredients
- A moderate to slow feel that should be maintained throughout.
- A I-IV-V chord progression with all seventh chords that characterizes the harmonic structure.
- A fluctuation between the major and minor 3rd of certain chords—the C and C♯ of an "A" chord. This can take place with any and all chords if desired.
- Tremolo effects that should be executed at a moderate speed (not too fast) to get the appropriate "lazy" feel.
- Bluesy fills that are to be played with the right hand while the left sets the groove. The melody is based on the "A" blues scale (A, C, D, E♭, E, G).

For Best Results
Dial up a classic honky-tonk or tack hammer piano sound.

Spice It Up
- Play behind the beat to make it even more sultry (and savory!).
- Swing it!

Sample the Recipes of These Leading Chefs of the Style
Son House, Skip James, Robert Johnson, Tommy Johnson, Charlie Patton, Bukka White.

TRACK 2

DELTA BLUES

JUMP BLUES

Most often comprised of driving rhythms, multi-horn voicings, and swaggering bellowed-out lyrics, the jazzy style known as jump blues was first popularized in the mid- to late-forties. Less guitar-oriented than the delta blues, jump is ideal for the keys, which can simulate the different instrumental elements of the style.

Time
4/4

Yield
Twelve measures of fast, jazz-tinged, jaunty, braggadocio blues.

Ingredients
- A fast swing tempo as opposed to the Delta.
- A repeated walking bass line played with the left hand in a 12-bar blues progression.
- A melody in simple solo style based on the B-flat blues scale (B♭, D♭, E♭, E, F, A♭).
- As with the Delta Blues, the same alternation between the major and minor 3rd of certain chords.

For Best Result
Use a classic honky-tonk piano sound or simulate the genuine jump blues sound of early recordings by using reverb on a medium "hall" setting.

Spice It Up
- Play the treble part of the melody with a sax sound dialed in (but choose this ingredient wisely; some synth-based sax sounds may be too cheesy).
- Add a dash of right-hand tremolo on the last chord.

Sample the Recipes of These Leading Chefs of the Style
Tiny Bradshaw, Nappy Brown, Roy Brown, Dr. John, Jay McShann, Amos Milburn, Roy Milton, Big Joe Turner.

JUMP BLUES

ROCKIN' BLUES

As its name implies, rockin' blues, or blues-rock, combines riff-heavy rock with shuffle-free, three-chord blues. During the 1970s, rockin' blues was nearly superceded by its spawn—the super amplified, guitar-dominated, anthem-laden "hard" rock. But blues-rock's power was restored the following decade when proponents returned to the style's bluesy roots.

Time
4/4

Yield
Twelve rockin' measures of shuffleless blues.

Ingredients
- Eighth notes that must be kept even—no shuffling!
- Alternating 5ths and 6ths (a la rhythm-guitar style) that drive the left hand.
- Chords that may be played staccato as desired, but try alternating between detached and legato phrasing.
- An ending (or, optionally, a turnaround to go back into it) that features a major/chromatic climb with the left hand to signal the end.
- A penultimate chord that chromatically leads to the last. Each pitch in the right hand moves a half-step down to resolve. Try this in any blues-based ending!

For Best Results
Dial in a standard piano sound with a tight slap-back delay effect to accentuate the rock 'n' roll feel.

Spice It Up
- Play this piece in a trio/quartet setting, being mindful that, if anyone solos over this pattern (guitar, sax, etc.), they should play sparsely.

Sample the Recipes of These Leading Chefs of the Style
The Allman Brothers Band, Eric Clapton, the Rolling Stones, Yardbirds, Johnny Winter, ZZ Top.

ROCKIN' BLUES

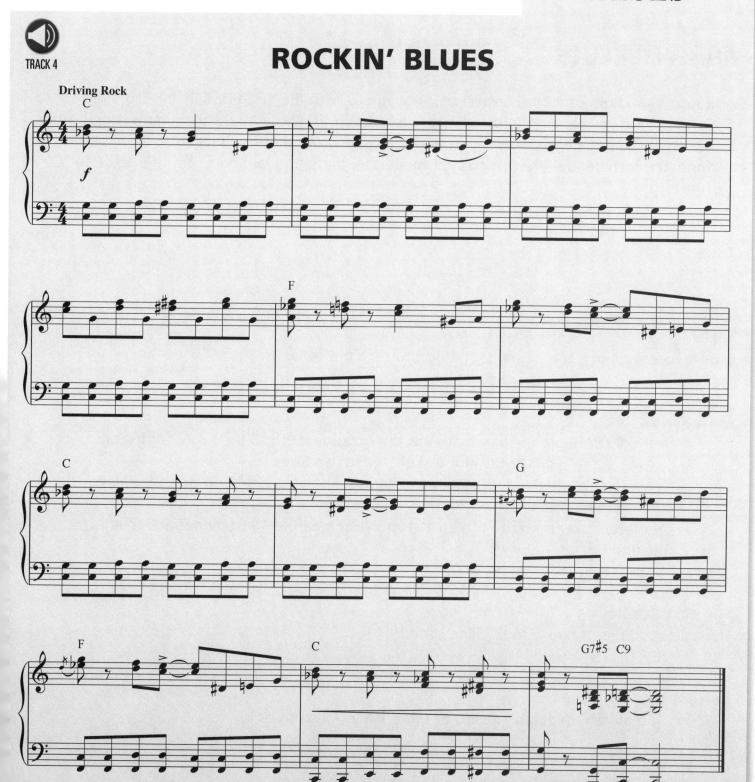

SHUFFLE BLUES

Although this idiom could be considered synonymous with the "traditional" blues genre ("shuffling" is a key element to the classic style), the shuffle blues really deserves recognition as its own style. Like the musical style that shares its name, the shuffle dance form should be performed nonchalantly—the tempo kept moderate, the swing laid-back, and the attitude perfunctory.

Time
4/4

Yield
Twelve measures of a traditional-sounding shuffle blues tune.

Ingredients
- A I-IV-V chord progression that adds the occasional 9th to the I & IV for flavor.
- A "swing" feel; adjust the amount of "swing" to taste.
- Similar to the rhythm guitar style in "Rockin' Blues," a left hand part that plays alternating 5ths and 6ths.
- Displaced accents on the triplets that occur in measure 10 to help signal that the end is near.

For Best Results
Use a classic blues or honky-tonk piano sound.

Spice It Up
- Add a dash of "room" reverb or tight delay (1 repetition).

Sample the Recipes of These Leading Chefs of the Style
Count Basie, Clarence "Gatemouth" Brown, Albert Collins, Duke Ellington, Freddie King, Howlin' Wolf, Memphis Slim, Professor Longhair, T-Bone Walker.

TRACK 5

SHUFFLE BLUES

SLOW (12/8) BLUES

The slow (12/8) blues is essentially a blues style that features an unhurried groove played in an easygoing manner. While perhaps not an "official" style of the blues genre, every blues musician considers it to be part of the blues establishment—one that all blues players should recognize and be capable of playing.

Time
12/8

Yield
Twelve measures of a 12-bar blues progression featuring a slow shuffle.

Ingredients
- Steady eighth notes that are to be played with the right hand, and a chord-outlining bass line played with the left.
- A shuffle in 12/8, meaning that the "swing" is inherent.
- Eighth notes that must not be rushed—if anything, put them "behind" the beat. The same goes for the bass line (think "laid-back" throughout).
- In this example, a bass line that carries the melodic interest. Bring it out.

For Best Results
Dial in an upright piano sound, with a slight detuning and "room" reverb. Do this without tack hammers or chorus, or the resulting sound could be too cheesy.

Spice It Up
- Add a slight crescendo to the I chord in measure 3 as a tension-building device to lead to the IV chord.
- Play an occasional C-sharp grace note before the left hand "Ds" in the first and third lines.

Sample the Recipes of These Leading Chefs of the Style
Buddy Guy, Albert King, B.B. King, Otis Spann, Stevie Ray Vaughan, T-Bone Walker, Muddy Waters.

TRACK 6

SLOW BLUES
(12/8)

BLUEGRASS

Firmly rooted in the country genre, bluegrass is the harder, faster scion of conventional string-band country. Pioneered by Bill Monroe and his band, the Blue Grass Boys, the idiom that is considered "traditional bluegrass" has remained unchanged since its inception in the 1940s. Although largely a string-dominated form, the often technically complex phrasings are easily translatable by keyboards.

Time
4/4

Yield
Eight measures of a country-blues variation featuring a simple chord progression that is meant to be played fast.

Ingredients
- A light and bouncy right hand on the repeated 16th notes to achieve a string instrument effect.
- A bright tempo that should not be allowed to drag.
- A simple chord progression—I, IV, V.
- A left hand part that plays the root and root/5th alternately.
- Slapped-out, right-hand sixteenths and eighths, and the occasional tangy grace note to move things along.
- A final eighth note that should be hit hard and staccato.

For Best Results
Use a straight-ahead piano sound with no obtrusive effects.

Spice It Up
- Speed up the repeating patterns a little more each time through until you're at a burning point!
- Incorporate a "pickin' and grinnin'" banjo or steel guitar over the pattern.

Sample the Recipes of These Leading Chefs of the Style
The Country Gentlemen, Lester Flatt, Earl Scruggs, the Kentucky Colonels, Bill Monroe, the Osbourne Brothers, the Stanley Brothers.

TRACK 7

BLUEGRASS

CLASSIC COUNTRY

Perhaps the most recognizable characteristic of classic, or traditional country is its signature twang. Likewise, its unfussy instrumentation and down-home lyrics reflect the rural life that inspired the style. Having since branched off into myriad spin-offs since its commercial debut in the early 1930s, classic country was, for decades, the mainstay of that institutional icon of country music, The Grand Ole Opry.

Time
4/4

Yield
Sixteen measures of pure country tradition.

Ingredients
- A slow to moderate tempo played straight—don't swing!
- A major, non-bluesy key to help enhance the positive classic country style.
- Chromatic motion between the I, IV, and V chords via the use of colorful triads.
- A lilting bass line that often alternates between the root and 5th of the chord.

For Best Results
Dial in a straight honky-tonk piano sound.

Spice It Up
- Add grace notes and trills in the right-hand chords.
- Try a Rhodes sound with a subtle tremolo effect.

Sample the Recipes of These Leading Chefs of the Style
Roy Acuff, Eddy Arnold, Johnny Cash, Patsy Cline, Red Foley, Tennessee Ernie Ford, Don Gibson, Willie Nelson, Ray Price, Jimmie Rodgers.

CLASSIC COUNTRY

CONTEMPORARY COUNTRY

Infused with rock, pop, and other crossover-friendly styles, contemporary country has, nonetheless, remained true to its traditional country roots. The "New Traditionalists," as the pioneers of this genre are known, developed this modern, yet authentic style by incorporating into its largely honky-tonk foundation, mass-market appeal, pop-rock elements, and current recording techniques. The result: Contemporary country is by far the most commercially successful style of the country music genre.

Time
4/4

Yield
Nine measures of a jazz- and R&B-influenced chord progression, the ingredient that gives this mix of country its contemporary sound.

Ingredients
- A moderate tempo, but not too slow (or the result would be a torch song!).
- Grace notes on the 2nd of a chord resolve to the 3rd. This is a signature country element (try it on a blues tune and you suddenly have a country flavor).
- A lightly played feel is essential; don't exaggerate any dynamics.

For Best Results
Use a piano or Rhodes sound.

Spice It Up
- Add a light chorus effect to your Rhodes sound for variety.
- Play some of the right-hand chords with Floyd Kramer-esque "backwards arpeggiations" (start them on the highest note and roll downwards).

Sample the Recipes of These Leading Chefs of the Style
Alabama, Garth Brooks, Roseanne Cash, Alan Jackson, the Judds, Toby Keith, Reba McEntire, George Strait, Randy Travis, Shania Twain.

TRACK 9

CONTEMPORARY COUNTRY

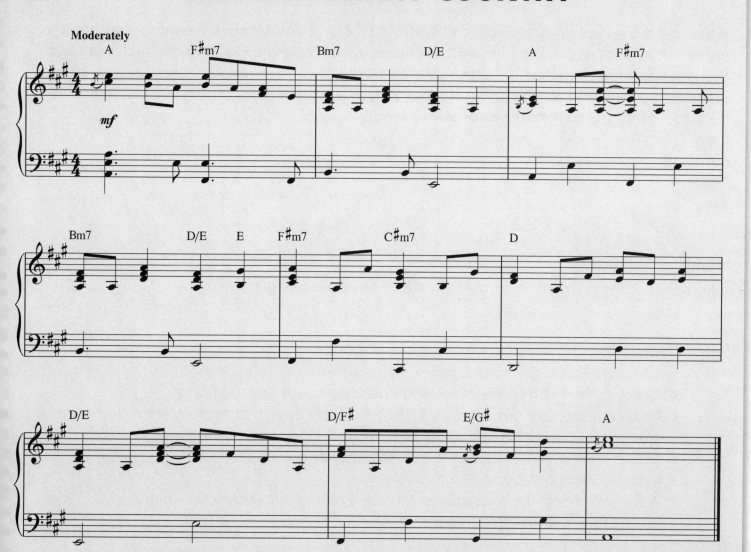

HOEDOWN

Hoedown is a mix of uptempo folk and Western swing—a combination meant to get the rural dancehall patrons of pre-World War II Americans out of their chairs and onto the dance floor. Perhaps less innovative than its jazz counterpart Dixieland, hoedown, in its heyday, served a primarily utilitarian function. Rather than serving as a creative outlet for musicians, hoedown was most often the backdrop for square dancing.

Time
2/4

Yield
Twelve high-energy measures of pure square-dance-era nostalgia.

Ingredients
- A four-measure intro that acts like a kick-off or a call to dancers.
- Opening right-hand 5ths to simulate the open strings on the fiddle.
- An accent on beat 1 of measure 3; the next three chords are softer, with Western-style grace notes played while the left hand ascends into the main pattern.
- "Boom-chik" style to be played with the left hand.
- Keep the tempo steady and danceable.
- In the last chord, the arpeggiated left hand, along with the octave-higher right, add finality (don't forget to tip your hat!).

For Best Results
Use an old-time, upright piano sound with tack hammers and slight detuning.

Spice It Up
- Play as a duet with fiddle (and maybe a drummer with brushes on a snare).

Sample the Recipes of These Leading Chefs of the Style
Millie Dillmount, Don Durlacher, Ray Flick, Slim Jackson & The Promenaders, Tommy Jackson, Dick Meyers.

TRACK 10

HOEDOWN

HONKY-TONK

Borrowing largely from the idioms of classic country—string instrumentation, nasalized vocals, and simple musical arrangements—honky-tonk's originality lies primarily in its heartbreak-and-hangover motif. Inspired by the tavern-dwelling lifestyle of the genre's original audience, honky-tonk has been a country music staple since its debut circa World War II. In addition, it served as the basis for other styles such as contemporary, progressive, and outlaw country.

Time
4/4

Yield
Eight measures of 12-bar-blues-based honky-tonk as popularized in the eponymous music halls across America.

Ingredients
- Tight staccato bass notes and playful, right-hand embellishments (grace notes, trills) to provide honky-tonk color.
- A root and 5th-style left hand to drive the music.
- Blues scale-based melodies that include the move from the minor 3rd to the major 3rd of a triad, often executed through the use of grace notes.
- Trills that occur on syncopated notes in the melody.

For Best Results
Dial in (what else?) a honky-tonk piano sound.

Spice It Up
- Swing the eighth notes!
- Try a tack hammer or Rhodes piano sound.

Sample the Recipes of These Leading Chefs of the Style
Merle Haggard; Lefty Frizzell; George Jones; Buck Owens; Fred Rose; Floyd Tillman; Ernest Tubb; Hank Williams, Sr.; Tammy Wynette.

TRACK 11

HONKY-TONK

BEBOP

Bebop (or just "bop") is jazz's "art" genre. Its emphasis of chords over melody as the improvisational framework was, at the height of the style's development, both revolutionary and radical. Nonetheless, bop is foundational to a plethora of jazz-genre spin-offs: hard bop, neo bop, cool jazz, to name a few. Thus, what was once a commercial albatross is now a jazz institution.

Time
4/4

Yield
Sixteen measures of a medium swing.

Ingredients
- Left-hand chords that are often used to accent and punctuate the right-hand melody, rather than just provide accompaniment for it.
- Heavy chromaticism and the use of large harmonies such as 11th and 13th chords characterize the progression.
- Ambiguous tonal center (what key is this tune in?!).
- Right-hand triplets played evenly, or with slight emphasis on the first note of each grouping.
- A relaxed energy should dominate; it is important in bebop to play with a natural, swinging feel without rigidity.

For Best Results
Use an acoustic grand piano sound with optional "room" or "hall" reverb—but no tack hammers or detuning! Also, make liberal use of the damper pedal.

Spice It Up
- Best served in a jazz trio setting with upright bass and drumset.

Sample the Recipes of These Leading Chefs of the Style
Dizzy Gillespie, Hank Jones, Thelonious Monk, Charlie Parker, Bud Powell, Sonny Stitt.

BEBOP

COOL JAZZ

Cool jazz became known as "West Coast" jazz due to its L.A.-based pioneers. While maintaining some of the artsy experimentation of bebop, cool jazz was often more moody and subdued. The "cool" comes from a more emotionless style, one that is more composed with less improvisation. Cool jazz was also influenced by contemporary classical composers like Stravinsky and Bartok. By 1960, however, it was largely displaced in mainstream jazz culture by its main rival, hard bop.

Time
Cut time (2/2)

Yield
Eight measures of a simple, laid-back, but lightly swinging structure that features large, often dissonant harmonies.

Ingredients
- An alternation between minor 11th harmonies on the I and IV chords.
- Sustained bass notes (pedal tones) to help accentuate the moodiness.
- Syncopation between the bass notes and the chords should be kept subtle and unexaggerated.
- Use pedal to help the rich harmonies ring out.

For Best Results
Dial in a standard grand piano sound.

Spice It Up
- Play in a jazz trio or quartet setting (piano, bass, sax, and drums with the drummer using brushes).
- Don the optional thin tie and horn-rimmed glasses. Capture the total "cool cat" vibe!

Sample the Recipes of These Leading Chefs of the Style
Chet Baker, Dave Brubeck, Miles Davis, Bill Evans, Gil Evans, Stan Getz, Vince Guaraldi, John Lewis, Gerry Mulligan, Jim Hall, Lenny Tristano.

TRACK 13

JAZZ

COOL JAZZ

DIXIELAND

Although named after the southern heartland where it originated, Dixieland was nurtured by the jazz musicians of 1920s Chicago (hence the style's other nickname, "Chicago jazz"). Having fallen out of favor with the genre's purists after its 1950s revival reduced it to a commercial cliché, Dixieland nonetheless maintains a strong popularity today.

Time
Cut time (2/2)

Yield
Thirty-two measures of a lively, popular, traditional tune.

Ingredients
- A bouncy and lively feel should be maintained throughout.
- Chromaticism can be used to connect one chord to another via the use of diminished and augmented chords.
- Most of this recipe calls for the left hand to bounce 1-5 bass notes on beats 1 and 3, while the right hand adds chord stabs on beat 2 amidst the sparse melody.

For Best Results
Use a tack hammer, standard upright, or old-time piano sound, with heavy emphasis on the mid-range, and incorporate some "room" or "hall" reverb. Detuning is okay.

Spice It Up
- Play in a duo/trio setting (just a snare with brushes is sufficient accompaniment; upright bass optional).

Sample the Recipes of These Leading Chefs of the Style
Louis Armstrong, Sidney Bechet, Bix Beiderbecke, Doc Cheatham, Pete Fountain, Turk Murphy, Muggsy Spanier, Jack Teagarden, Lu Watters.

DIXIELAND

TRACK 14

HARD BOP

Having evolved in the 1950s and '60s from its predecessor, bebop, the "hard" version of the genre is more or less the antithesis of its rival cool (or West Coast) jazz. Hard bop is looser, simpler, and even a bit gospel-and R&B-influenced. Due to the growing appeal of fusion, as well as the loss of hard bop's official record label Blue Note, the style's popularity had waned considerably by 1970. However, hard bop did experience a renaissance of sorts in the 1980s, and is still preserved today by the genre's traditionalists.

Time
4/4

Yield
Twelve measures of bebop's simpler, looser, and perhaps more soulful cousin.

Ingredients
- Maintain a high-energy feel throughout.
- A simple bass line and melody with abundant rhythmic repetition to keep things loose.
- A simple chord progression revolving around the I and IV chords.
- Accent the repetitive syncopation on the "and" of beat 4, every other measure.

For Best Results
Dial in a standard grand piano sound.

Spice It Up
- Best when played in a trio setting (piano, bass, drums) or quartet (piano, bass, drums, and sax).

Sample the Recipes of These Leading Chefs of the Style
Nat Adderley, Art Blakey, Sonny Clark, John Coltrane, Kenny Dorham, Lee Morgan, Wayne Shorter, Horace Silver, Bobby Timmons, McCoy Tyner.

TRACK 15

HARD BOP

Moderately (no swing)

RAGTIME

Much like Dixieland and stride, ragtime is essentially the interaction between bouncing bass notes and chords in the left hand, and a contrasting melody in the right. The result is that, compared to stride or Dixieland, the ragtime style sounds a bit more aristocratic, dense, and composed.

Time
Cut time (2/2)

Yield
Sixteen measures of the quintessential ragtime tune, "The Entertainer."

Ingredients
- A restrained energy dominates. The feel is bouncy and happy, but not frenetic.
- A syncopated melody via the use of an eighth-quarter-eighth rhythmic pattern.
- Both left- and right-hand parts to be played evenly and steadily. It's easy to speed up on syncopated parts like this, but ragtime calls for an unvarying rhythm—no Swing!
- The left hand bounces back and forth as in stride piano.
- The turnaround (measure 13) requires a slight increase in energy.
- A bottom voice that executes a chromatic descent, preparing for the end.

For Best Results
Use tack hammers and slight detuning if desired, with slight reverb being optional (roll off some treble if the sound is too harsh).

Spice It Up
- Ideally, play with a full brass band! However, until you can afford that, snare-with-brushes accompaniment is sufficient.

Sample the Recipes of These Leading Chefs of the Style
Dick Baker, Eubie Blake, Rube Bloom, Scott Joplin, Sue Keller, Joe Lamb, Max Morath, Jelly Roll Morton, John Mooney, Joshua Rifkin.

TRACK 16

RAGTIME

By Scott Joplin

STRIDE

Unlike many of the other musical idioms presented in this book, stride is a piano-dominant style. Much akin to ragtime in structure, but with a looser, swingier feel, stride piano features percussive left-hand "oom-pahs" and right-hand melodic and harmonic improvisations. It remains one of modern jazz's biggest influences.

Time
4/4

Yield
Eight measures plus a four-measure introduction of a moderately swung, eighth-note shuffle pattern.

Ingredients
- A feel that is steady and relaxed throughout—"stride," don't stumble.
- A crescendo and left-hand descending motion to help build the introduction leading into the main theme.
- The left hand bounces back and forth from the lower- to mid-register in steady quarter notes while the right hand plays a highly ornamented, chordal melody on top. Keep this steady and practice the left hand by itself before adding the melody.
- Ornamentation includes grace notes in measures 4, 5, and 11, and fast triplets in measure 9.
- Exaggerate the dynamics at the end. Play softly in the second-to-last measure, then very loud on the last chord (and don't forget to take a bow!).

For Best Results
Dial in a standard, old-time piano sound.

Spice It Up
- Simulate an old stride recording with high mids, "room" reverb, and slight detuning.

Sample the Recipes of These Leading Chefs of the Style
James P. Johnson, Lucky Roberts, Willie "The Lion" Smith, Art Tatum, Joe Turner, Thomas "Fats" Waller, Teddy Wilson.

STRIDE

TRACK 17

BOLERO

As its name (which means "ballad") implies, bolero is a romantic, emotive Latin American style that arose in Cuba in the late nineteenth century, and was widespread by the 1950s. Never completely out of the picture, bolero experienced a significant renaissance in the 1990s, as the young balladeers of the flourishing Latin-pop market cashed in on the style's passionate spirit.

Time
4/4

Yield
Ten measures plus a four-measure introduction of the Latin American counterpart to the torch song.

Ingredients
- A quiet mood (remember, "ballad") that should be maintained throughout (except for the dramatic-contrast accents where indicated).
- A signature triplet motif played by the right hand (one right-hand finger plays and holds the upper voice notes while the thumb beats out the triplets).
- A subtle, march-like rhythm that should be maintained by the left hand (1, rest, 3, 4...).
- An ending that features a forte descent at the end of measure 12 to be played with both hands. Accent beat 1 of measure 13, then play the right-hand triplets softly.
- The final notes are to be played full force.

For Best Results
Dial in a standard piano sound.

Spice It Up
- Try as a duet with a flute or a clarinet playing the melody (a la Ravel's "Bolero"), or a snare drum playing the march-style ostinato.

Sample the Recipes of These Leading Chefs of the Style
Roberto Carlos, Augustin Lara, Luis Miguel, Beny Moré, Daniel Santos, Los Tres Diamantes, Trio Los Panchos, Charlie Zaa.

BOLERO

BOSSA NOVA

Bossa nova is a combination of light Brazilian rhythms and cool (West Coast) jazz. Developed in the 1950s, the style was inculcated into American culture primarily by way of the 1959 film *Black Orpheus*, which was scored by bossa nova pioneer, composer Antonio Carlos Jobim. The style reached its pinnacle in the 1960s, helped by the hugely successful 1964 song, "Girl from Ipanema."

Time
4/4

Yield
A 20-measure, standard Latin progression. (The bossa nova is often more complex than the other Latin styles featured in this book in terms of chords and left-hand/right-hand complexity.)

Ingredients
- A medium pace and steady tempo.
- A repetitious rhythmic pattern in the left hand. Keep it steady; imagine a Latin percussion section backing you up.
- A tricky right-hand part plays both the melody and accompaniment as independent elements.
- Extended (7, 9, 11, etc...) and altered (♭5, ♯5, etc...) chords and chromatic progressions similar to those in bebop and cool jazz.

For Best Results
Dial in a standard piano sound.

Spice It Up
- If you can split the keyboard, go for a Caribbean flavor by dialing in a right-hand marimba-type sound.

Sample the Recipes of These Leading Chefs of the Style
Luiz Bonfa, Charlie Byrd, Stan Getz, Astrud Gilberto, João Gilberto, Antonio Carlos Jobim.

BOSSA NOVA

TRACK 19

CHA-CHA

The history of the cha-cha is a bit vague: it was either a reinvention of the mambo (hence, its nickname, the "double mambo") or a style that arose from the Cuban *danzón*—dance popular among late-nineteenth century Cuban high society. By the early 1950s, the Latin craze had invaded American dance halls, and the cha-cha became a staple in every populist orchestra's repertoire.

Time
4/4

Yield
Eight measures of a bright, Latin progression featuring a simple I-V-I-IV-I-V-I chord progression.

Ingredients
- A bright, steady tempo that should be maintained throughout.
- A simple progression that allows the player to concentrate on articulation and feel. Play it bouncy and in the pocket.
- A left-hand bass part, rhythmically similar to the rhumba, but busier.
- Rhythm is the key! Both the right and left hands have their own rhythmic motives that repeat throughout—these give the cha-cha its character.
- A melody harmonized in parallel thirds.
- The end rhythm: "CHA CHA CHA!" Feel free to shout it out.

For Best Results
Dial in a standard piano sound.

Spice It Up
- Incorporate a full Latin ensemble, or at the very least, some maracas!

Sample the Recipes of These Leading Chefs of the Style
Al Castellanos, Xavier Cugat, Henri Debs, Ninón Mondejar y su Orquestra America, Orquestra Aragón, Alex Torres, René Touzet.

CHA-CHA

MERENGUE

Merengue arose in the mid-nineteenth century as the eponymous backdrop of a popular Dominican Republic peasant-class folk dance. A mix of Spanish and African influences, the style traditionally featured prominent vocals as well as accordion, guitar, drum, and marimba. Later, the accordion was supplanted by synthesizers and electric guitar, which today are considered merengue-ensemble essentials.

Time
Cut time (2/2)

Yield
Seventeen measures (including the repeat) of the official national music of the Dominican Republic.

Ingredients
- A bouncy feel that should be maintained throughout. Don't swing it, play with a relaxed energy.
- A syncopated melody similar to ragtime.
- A sparse and simple bass line consisting of the root and 5th of each chord. This helps provide for a solid pulse that the right-hand syncopation can play off of.
- A punctuated ending should be especially adhered to if playing with an ensemble.

For Best Results
Dial in a standard piano sound.

Spice It Up
- Play along with a 2-3 clave pattern (programmed or live).

Sample the Recipes of These Leading Chefs of the Style
Alex Bueno, Manny Manuel, New York Band, Oro Solido, Tõno Rosario, Los Toros Band, Sergio Vargas, Johnny Ventura.

MERENGUE

Moderately, in 2

RHUMBA

The rhumba which is actually a phonetically identical, but highly Anglicized knock-off of the Cuban "rumba," was developed by big-band leaders eager to please scores of Americans who flocked to Havana nightclubs to evade Prohibition. They returned only to demand more of their beloved Cuban music.

Time
4/4

Yield
Eleven measures of a moderately fast progression featuring a 3-measure intro.

Ingredients
- A steady groove that is not swung.
- A 3-measure intro that establishes the groove and sets up the pattern with detached syncopation.
- Beat 4 of the left hand should always be held for full-value. A slight accent is optional.
- A left-hand rhythm that repeats itself each measure is essential to the style.
- A strong ending chord—emphasizing the silence right before it helps to end the piece with a bang!

For Best Results
Use a standard grand piano sound with no effects.

Spice It Up
- Since this is in a 3-2 clave, have one playing along, if possible.

Sample the Recipes of These Leading Chefs of the Style
Xaviar Cugat, Rubén Gonzáles, Beny Moré, Los Munequitos de Matanzas, Orquestra de La Playa, Pancho Quinto.

RHUMBA

SAMBA

Although there are a number of African-influenced Brazilian music idioms that fall under the umbrella term "samba," the most common form is the dance music popularized by Carnival. Samba also features elements of the batuque (Brazilian-Portuguese music and dance) tradition, the characteristics of which most modern samba Westernizers tend to emphasize over those of African influence.

Time
4/4

Yield
Twenty measures of a fast groove in the spirit of Carnival.

Ingredients
- A groove played fast and evenly.
- A left hand that establishes the pulse with quarter notes on beats 1 and 3. The right-hand melody employs a repetitious syncopation. Accent the "and" of beat two.
- A harmonic progression that revolves around the I, II, and V, chords with a bridge of sorts in the second-to-last line.

For Best Results
Use a standard piano sound.

Spice It Up
- Add a touch of funk by incorporating an electric piano or a clavinet sound.

Sample the Recipes of These Leading Chefs of the Style
Alcione, Jorge Ben, Dorival Caymmi, Gal Costa, Martinho Da Vila, Carmen Miranda, Leila Pinhiero.

TRACK 23

SAMBA

TANGO

With its syncopated, yet repetitious, bass line, the tango was obviously made for dancing! Despite its wild popularity in America and Europe circa World War I, the tango—which incites closely intertwined couples to sweep passionately across dancehall floors—was considered so sultry that it was banned by both the German Kaiser Wilhelm II and Pope Pius X.

Time
4/4

Yield
Ten measures plus a two-measure introduction of the popular dance music that features the style's signature minor mode (in this case, D minor).

Ingredients
- A bass line that begins the tune and establishes its characteristic dance rhythm.
- Articulations and slurs should be followed carefully to promote the tango style.
- A right-hand melody harmonized predominantly by parallel thirds.

For Best Results
Use a straight piano sound.

Spice It Up
- Accent the first left-hand note of each measure.
- Play as a duet with either an accordion or a violin.

Sample the Recipes of These Leading Chefs of the Style
Osvaldo Berlingieri, Enrique Chia, Silvana Deluigi, Carlos Gardel, Alberto Gomez, Astor Piazzolla.

TANGO

CLASSIC ROCK

The successor of the album rock idiom that dominated the FM-radio airwaves in the 1970s, classic rock has become a catch-all for a number of album-oriented styles—heavy metal, blues-rock, Southern rock, and prog-rock, to name a few. The true ties that bind classic rock, however, are the blue-collar ideology reflected in its lyrics, the "workin' for the weekend" drive of its music, and the arena-worthy power of its performance.

Time
4/4

Yield
Four repeated measures of a moderate, straight-ahead groove that features a I-VII-IV-I progression reminiscent of pure, good-time, BTO-esque rock 'n' roll.

Ingredients
- Syncopated melody, but not swing. Play aggressively!
- Blues-based chord progression dominated by seventh chords.
- A left-hand part that emulates guitar power chords through harmonic fifths and sixths. Play these with force.
- A repetitious rhythmic figure in the left hand to give the tune its drive.

For Best Results
Dial in either a standard or electric piano sound with no effects.

Spice It Up
- Play in a rock trio (keyboards, bass, and drums) or quartet (keyboards, bass, drums, and guitar) setting.

Sample the Recipes of These Leading Chefs of the Style
Aerosmith, Bachman-Turner Overdrive, Bad Company, the Doobie Brothers, Grand Funk Railroad, the James Gang, Tom Petty, Bob Seger.

TRACK 25

CLASSIC ROCK

Driving Rock

DISCO

Short for "discotheque"—the dance clubs that spawned the style—disco has for a foundation the 1970s R&B groove styles like soul and funk. The incorporation of pop hooks led to disco's phenomenal radio and record sales success. This encouraged acts of all conceivable idioms to record their own disco records.

Time
4/4

Yield
Eight repeated measures, plus a 4-measure intro of a Hustle-inciting groove.

Ingredients
- A right-hand part that acts like a horn section, with left-hand octaves like a bass guitar. The intro serves as a fanfare, calling dancers to the floor. The accented triplets in measure 3 help to build this momentum.
- Accents on the lower octaves that lock in with a hypothetical bass drum playing on "all fours."
- A metronomic pulse, without variation, should be maintained throughout.
- Exaggerate the staccato in the right hand to sound like a tight and punchy horn section.

For Best Results
Use either an electric or acoustic piano sound (chorus or phase effects are acceptable), or even synth-horns.

Spice It Up
- Play with a full band (keyboards, bass, drums, guitar, plus optional horns)—the ideal setting for this style.

Sample the Recipes of These Leading Chefs of the Style
The Bee Gees, Chic, K.C. & The Sunshine Band, Sister Sledge, Donna Summer, Village People.

DISCO

EARLY ROCK 'N' ROLL

Influenced by blues, country, folk, gospel, jazz, and R&B, early rock 'n' roll featured hooky melodies and a dance-friendly backbeat. It combined these beloved musical elements in a novel, engaging way, setting off a host of subsequent idioms such as British Invasion, punk, heavy metal, hard rock, and glam.

Time
4/4

Yield
Sixteen measures of a fast, swinging, rock 'n' roll classic.

Ingredients
- A shuffle feel that should be maintained throughout. Swing those eighth notes!
- "Power chords" to be banged out by the left hand. Keep these steady; they should mimic a rhythm guitar.
- A melody harmonized in full chords for the verse played by the right hand.
- A right-hand chorus melody that alternates with the "tweet, tweet" chords in the upper register. Accent these and keep the left hand steady while you play the syncopated hits.
- Double-handed, full-force hits that comprise the ending. Note that the left-hand octaves in the last measure hit after the fermata (in free time, so if you're playing with a band, someone must cue this final hit).

For Best Results
Dial in a standard piano sound. A tight slap-back delay or "room" reverb is okay.

Spice It Up
- Play in a trio (keyboards, bass, and drums) or quartet (keyboards, bass, drums, and guitar or sax) setting.

Sample the Recipes of These Leading Chefs of the Style
Chuck Berry, Bo Diddley, the Everly Brothers, Bill Haley & The Comets, Buddy Holly & The Crickets, Jerry Lee Lewis, Little Richard, Elvis Presley, the Shirelles.

EARLY ROCK 'N' ROLL

Words and Music by
J. THOMAS

TRACK 27

NEW AGE

Developed as a means for linking mind, body, and spirit, New Age music was meant to be atmospheric, meditative, and therapeutic. Since its emergence in the 1970s, the genre has branched into sub-styles including progressive electronic, neo-classical, ethnic fusion, techno-tribal, space, ambient, and healing.

Time
Cut time (2/2)

Yield
Twelve measures plus a two-measure introduction of aesthetically appealing mood music.

Ingredients
- A smooth damper pedal technique is integral. Lift on beat 1 of each measure, and depress again on the next beat.
- The pulse can be ambiguous. Take your time and be free.
- The repetitious left-hand pattern should not be varied while the right plays its sparse, peaceful melody on top. The melody should "sing" freely above.
- Exaggerate the ritard at the end; let it ring.

For Best Results
Use a grand piano sound with reverb or long delay; if available, mix with a sustaining string-synth sound.

Spice It Up
- Try as a duet with a harp, flute, or other soft instrument.
- Take your keyboard outside and play in the woods.

Sample the Recipes of These Leading Chefs of the Style
Jim Brickman, Enya, Exchange, Jean Michael Jarre, Kitaro, David Lanz, Liz Story, John Tesh, George Winston, Yanni.

NEW AGE

POP ROCK

Bright, hooky, clean, and polished are the primary characteristics of pop rock music. Relying heavily on tight recording techniques to capture its essence and distinguish it as a distinct style in its own right, pop rock features such pure rock elements as a driving backbeat and controlled high-energy edginess. The style emerged in the 1960s, but really came into its own in the 1970s. Today, it remains a viable force in contemporary music culture.

Time
4/4

Yield
Twelve measures of a moderated, syncopated, catchy groove.

Ingredients
- After a four-measure intro, the upper voice of the right hand plays a catchy melody—the all-important "hook" present in pop music.
- The right hand establishes a steady pulse while the left grooves with syncopation.
- A non-blues chord progression. Harmony extends beyond I, IV, V, and takes advantage of VI chords as well as suspensions and extensions (7ths and 9ths).

For Best Results
Choose from a number of sound options: standard piano, electric piano, synth-horns, fast-attack strings, or a split sound (i.e., electric piano in the left, synth in the right).

Spice It Up
- Accent the first beat of measure 1 on the repeat.
- Play with a full rock band (keyboards, bass, drums, and guitar) and create your own lyrics for the melody to sing along.

Sample the Recipes of These Leading Chefs of the Style
Carpenters, Hall & Oates, Bruce Hornsby, Michael Jackson, Billy Joel, Elton John, Prince, Sting.

POP ROCK

REGGAE

While its origin may be Jamaican, reggae's pedigree is pure New Orleanian. In the 1960s, Jamaican musicians were enthralled with the New Orleans R&B played on American radio programs. As a result, they developed their own uptempo derivation of this rhythm 'n' blues, which they called "ska." Shortly thereafter, perhaps due to the inherent mellowness of Jamaican culture, ska's beat was tempered. The result was the laid-back feel that is now the heart of reggae's sound.

Time
Cut time (2/2)

Yield
Eight measures of a moderate, laid-back, rootsy shuffle featuring a standard I-IV-I-V reggae progression.

Ingredients
- A standard reggae progression with chords that should not be overly colored with extensions.
- Accent beat two (cut-time) of each measure. This will simulate the placement of the bass drum which is important to the reggae groove.
- A right-hand rhythmic accompaniment that is also essential to the groove, filling the spaces between the bass line. Play slightly behind the beat.
- A bouncy, yet laid-back feel should prevail.

For Best Results
Use an electric piano or, if available, a Hammond B3 organ sound.

Spice It Up
- Play in a full rock band (keyboards, bass, drums, guitar, and horns) setting.

Sample the Recipes of These Leading Chefs of the Style
Buju Banton, Don Carlos, Eddie Grant, Bob Marley & The Wailers, Ziggy Marley & The Melody Makers, Freddie McGregor, Peter Tosh, UB40, Bunny Wailer.

REGGAE

CONTEMPORARY R&B

Since debuting in the 1990s—when the production-slick styles of dance-R&B and hip-hop began infiltrating the sounds of classic rhythm 'n' blues—contemporary R&B has maintained the urban polish that set it apart from the traditional style that spawned it. However, in recent years, a number of the style's artists have been re-infusing the idiom with classic elements from traditional R&B and soul.

Time
4/4

Yield
Twelve measures of a fresh, stylish, and refined rendering of R&B.

Ingredients
- A slow, laid-back tempo is imperative to the proper R&B feel. Play it too fast and it becomes a rock or pop tune.
- The minor key, dominated by seventh chords, helps establish the serious, yet fun mood.
- A more complex chord progression than common to most traditional blues.
- Syncopated lines emphasizing the "and" of beat two in both hands.

For Best Results
Use an electric piano sound with some synth strings, if possible.

Spice It Up
- Repeat the last chord an octave higher after holding the original last chord for 2-4 beats.
- Accent the C#dim7 at beat 4 of measure 2.

Sample the Recipes of These Leading Chefs of the Style
Erykah Badu, D'Angelo, Terence Trent D'Arby, Craig David, Macy Gray, Lauryn Hill, India.Arie, Wyclef Jean, Alicia Keys, Maxwell, Jill Scott.

CONTEMPORARY R&B

FUNK

More greatly influenced by African musical elements than any other style of the R&B genre, funk is often more polyrhythmic, more unstructured, and more organically primal than other R&B-derived idioms. Coming into its own in the 1960s, funk (a slang word meaning "stink," in reference to its raw earthiness) compositions are likely to bypass, or rework conventional song structure, and instead highlight extended, groove-heavy jams and improvisations.

Time
4/4

Yield
Twelve measures (including the repeat) of the R&B genre's most primal spin-off.

Ingredients
- A catchy, rhythmic bass line is important. Here, a strong, staccato quarter note on the tonic (D) helps kick off almost every measure.
- Play the left hand louder than the right and bring out the accents.
- Punctuate the right-hand staccato chords to simulate a horn section. End it with a strong accent and double the last note in the left hand an octave lower (a screamed, James Brown-style "Ow!" is optional).

For Best Results
Split your sound into a Hammond organ in the right hand, and piano in the left, if possible.

Spice It Up
- Add a varying-speed Leslie effect on the Hammond sound.
- Use a clavinet or slap-bass sound for the left hand.
- If you have a non-cheesy horn section sound, try substituting that for the Hammond sound in the right hand (but absolutely avoid the cheese!).

Sample the Recipes of These Leading Chefs of the Style
James Brown; George Clinton; Earth, Wind & Fire; Rick James; the Ohio Players; Parliament; Sly & The Family Stone; Tower of Power.

FUNK

GOSPEL R&B

With its foundation in African-American spirituals, the celebratory, hallelujah-evoking sounds of gospel have inspired the styles of doo-wop and contemporary Christian music. Comprised of elements from a variety of idioms—including country, blues, soul, and as of late, pop and even punk—gospel has today branched off into myriad different popular sub-styles such as inspirational, Christian rap, Christian comedy, and Jesus rock.

Time
4/4

Yield
Eight measures (plus pickup) of a rootsy, celebratory tune in the spirit of the African-American Southern gospel choirs.

Ingredients
- A low-simmer tempo that should dominate.
- A colorful chord progression that features extended triads (7ths and 9ths), altered chords (♭5), inverted (B♭7/D), and those which are chromatic (i.e., do not belong "naturally" in the key, such as the F♯dim7).
- Play it with feeling. Exaggerate the syncopations and articulations.
- Some grace notes are included, feel free to add your own.
- Bring out the rests in measures 3 and 7 by executing a very short staccato right before them.

For Best Results
Use a classic piano sound.

Spice It Up
- When you've got the groove down, experiment with different rhythm variations.
- Play it rubato (in free time), with plenty of expressive ritards and crescendos.
- To capture the rootsy feel, try a slightly out-of-tune piano sound.

Sample the Recipes of These Leading Chefs of the Style
The Anointed, the Brooklyn Tabernacle Choir, Shirley Caesar, Donnie McClurkin, Smokie Norful, Jubilant Sykes, Take 6, CeCe Winans.

GOSPEL R&B

MOTOWN

Named after the Detroit-based independent label that popularized its sound, Motown was largely the creation of record producer Berry Gordy, Jr.. Beginning in the 1960s, Gordy incorporated pop-rock hooks into traditional R&B. Eventually, a new sound was developed, one that was more accessible to, and commercially successful with, mainstream audiences. This accomplishment was something that other "black" idioms had not been able to achieve.

Time
Cut time (2/2)

Yield
Thirty-three measures of pop-infused, Detroit R&B.

Ingredients
- A right-hand part with a bouncy, energetic feel.
- The first sixteen bars serve as an introduction. The melody follows, accompained by virtually the same music as is sounded in the intro.
- A simple chord progression, one based on I, IV, V.
- To convey a more pop style, keep the tempo relatively fast.

For Best Results
Use a straight piano or Rhodes sound.

Spice It Up
- Try a Farfisa-style organ sound in the right hand.
- Add a spicy glissando to lead into each new section (example: the ends of measures 16 and 32.

Sample the Recipes of These Leading Chefs of the Style
The Four Tops, Marvin Gaye, the Jackson 5, Martha & The Vandellas, the Miracles, Diana Ross & the Supremes, the Temptations.

MOTOWN

TRACK 34

SOUL

Itself an amalgamation of musical elements such as pop-friendly Motown and rough-edged R&B, soul first emerged in the 1960s and inspired sub-idioms such as funk, disco, and urban music throughout the 1970s. Hooky, rootsy, gritty, and smooth, soul was a pop-crossover favorite until its evolution eventually became its demise. Although it rarely appears on the charts today, soul is still actively preserved by traditionalists.

Time
4/4

Yield
Seven measures of rhythm 'n' blues at its smoothest and catchiest.

Ingredients
- A moderate tempo (a la "Green Onions") throughout.
- Syncopations galore—be sure to groove consistently throughout. Bring out the staccato and accents.
- Observe and exaggerate the rests. They are important to the soulful feel.
- A simple and bluesy chord progression. Jazzier extended chords are used at the end for some flavor.

For Best Results
Dial in a Rhodes or Wurlitzer-style piano sound or a Hammond organ sound.

Spice It Up
- Add a varying-speed Leslie rotating speaker effect to your Hammond organ sound.
- Include percussion on all accented and staccato notes.

Sample the Recipes of These Leading Chefs of the Style
Booker T. & The MGs, Ray Charles, Sam Cooke, Aretha Franklin, Gladys Knight & The Pips, Al Green, Curtis Mayfield, Wilson Pickett, Otis Redding.

SOUL

TRACK 35

CLASSICAL

The expression "classical music" is perhaps most often associated with the formally structured compositions of the late eighteenth and early nineteenth centuries. However, if one looks at musical forms such as the art song and the symphony, as well as any "academic" music, the term "classical" can apply to that which dates back to the fourth century A.D. up to the present day. It is considered one of the oldest genres (not including folk) to arise from the European tradition.

Time
4/4

Yield
Eight measures of Mozart's classic "Sonata in C Major."

Ingredients
- A steady tempo throughout.
- The so-called "Alberti bass," as seen from the beginning in the left hand (root-fifth-third-fifth) is a trademark of the Mozart-era style.
- Scalar passages such as these included in the right hand in measures 5-7 are characteristic of the style and should be played as evenly as possible.
- A simple chord progression (I-IV-V).
- The right-hand trill in measure 4 should be played in fast repetitions, alternating between the E and F, with the first and second fingers. Such an ornament is common in this style.

For Best Results
Use a standard piano or harpsichord sound.

Spice It Up
- Add your own dynamic shading—crescendos and diminuendos.

Sample the Recipes of These Leading Chefs of the Style
Johann Sebastian Bach, Ludwig van Beethoven, Franz Joseph Haydn, Felix Mendelssohn, Wolfgang Amadeus Mozart, Franz Schubert.

CLASSICAL

Wolfgang Amadeus Mozart
1756-1891
K 545

FOLK

Folk music was born from the oral traditions that were carried out in Europe and America for centuries. It reflects in its characteristics, unfussy, acoustic-based, authorless traits, and the story-oriented simplicity of the common classes who originated it. During the 1960s, the genre was a favorite vehicle for topical songwriters, in particular, those with political agendas. Many of today's folk musicians include both old and new material in their repertoires. This is practiced in the hopes of both evolving the style and preserving the tradition.

Time
4/4

Yield
Ten measures (plus pickup) of a traditional American folk tune.

Ingredients
- Simple chord progression of mostly triads.
- Play it freely (we're not dancing to it!).
- Left-hand arpeggiated chords for extra expression.
- Make liberal use of the damper pedal. Lift and depress at every chord change.
- Add your own dynamics. The feel should be based on what your ears tell you (remember the oral tradition).

For Best Results
Use a standard, or old-time, piano sound, but no detuning or tack hammers—either of which would upset the subtlety of the tune.

Spice It Up
- Add your own grace notes by approaching important melody notes from a step or half step below.
- Try in a duet with a violin.

Sample the Recipes of These Leading Chefs of the Style
Joan Baez; Woodie Guthrie; Burl Ives; Kingston Trio; Alan Lomax; Peter, Paul & Mary; Pete Seeger; the Weavers.

FOLK

Tune: Shenandoah

Slowly, freely

With pedal

FOX TROT

Both the popular ballroom dance and accompanying musical style known as the Fox trot are named after their inventor, Vaudevillian actor, Harry Fox. During the summer of 1914, Fox was the music director for a famed cinema house that provided intermission-time entertainment—including a group of dancers who "trotted" to ragtime tunes. Before long, the phenomenally successful Fox trot had even supplanted dancehall mainstays like the popular two-step.

Time
4/4

Yield
Sixteen measures of a favorite, traditional, ballroom dance pattern.

Ingredients
- No syncopation or frills—play steady, straight ahead, and keep the dynamic *mezzo forte* throughout.
- A simple bass line that consists of half notes sounding the roots and fifths of the chords.
- Bring out the upper voice (melody) in the right hand. The notes underneath should be softer and accompanimental.
- Arpeggiate the last chord to let the dancers know the tune has ended.

For Best Results
Use a standard piano sound.

Spice It Up
- Put some breathing space between the half notes in the left hand to simulate the phrasing of a tuba or upright bass.

Sample the Recipes of These Leading Chefs of the Style
George & Ira Gershwin, Earl Hooker, Harry James, Glenn Miller, Palace Orchestra, Tuxedo Junction, Lawrence Welk.

FOX TROT

TRACK 38

POLKA

The polka (Czech for "half-step") hails from early eighteenth-century Bohemia where it originally accompanied a peasant dance of the same name. By the mid-nineteenth century, both the dance and the musical style were all the rage in Prague ballrooms. After its acceptance by Parisian audiences shortly thereafter, the polka became popular throughout all of Europe. Still beloved today, of all the dance forms to have emerged out of the nineteenth-century, the polka is the only one still thriving.

Time
4/4

Yield
Sixteen measures of a tune based on the traditional Northern European polka themes.

Ingredients
- High energy should be maintained throughout; stay on top of the beat.
- Left-hand "oom-pahs" that act like a tuba. Keep these steady and staccato as they're the backbone of the polka.
- The simple chord progression revolves around I-IV-V.

For Best Results
Use a standard piano sound.

Spice It Up
- If you repeat the whole progression, rest on beat 4 of measure 8.
- Speed the tempo up if you're familiar enough with the music.
- Try in a trio (drummer, on brushes, and bass) setting.

Sample the Recipes of These Leading Chefs of the Style
Brave Combo, Happy Glad Polka Band, Frankie Liszka & The Brass Connection, Jimmy Sturr, Lawrence Welk, Frankie Yankovic & His Yanks.

POLKA

TRACK 39

WALTZ

Waltz, from the Old German word *walzen* ("to glide or turn"), features the now immediately recognizable 3/4 time signature that urges couples to "one, two, three" their ways across ballroom floors the world over. Having originated among the peasants of Austria and Bavaria sometime before the seventeenth century, the dance form was embraced by the elite once waltz music made its way into the royal European courts. Made even more popular by the compositions of Franz Lanner and Johann Strauss, the waltz went on to become one of the most well-known and beloved of all ballroom dance styles.

Time
3/4

Yield
Sixteen measures (plus ending) of an excerpt of Strauss's "By the Beautiful Blue Danube" waltz.

For Best Results
Use a standard piano sound.

Ingredients
- A serene, gentle feel should be maintained throughout.
- Articulate the left hand as indicated to bring out the dance style.
- Make a contrast between the staccato and legato parts of the melody.
- Maintaining a waltz tempo throughout is important. If you can imagine yourself dancing to it, it will sound authentic.

Spice It Up
- Arpeggiate the right-hand staccato chords, where appropriate, if desired.

Sample the Recipes of These Leading Chefs of the Style
Joseph Lanner, Franz Leher, Andre Rieu, Sigmund Romberg, Johann Strauss II, Joseph Strauss, Emile Waldteufel, Carl Michael Ziehrer.

WALTZ

Johann Strauss, Jr.

THE AUTHOR

ABOUT THE AUTHOR

Jana Ranson is a published music-subject author who is also a freelance editor and copywriter for Hal Leonard. With an extensive background in the music business that has included stints in concert promotion, talent management and booking, nightclub operations, and radio, Jana brings a thorough understanding of the music industry to her writing projects. In 2003, her first publication, *The Hal Leonard Pocket Rhyming Dictionary* was released, and has since earned rave reviews. The *Keyboard Cookbook* is her second book for Hal Leonard. She currently lives in Milwaukee, Wisconsin.